Cepeda's atmospheric poems evoke an image of death that's horrific and lovely, which I believe is fundamentally an optimism. *We Are the Ones Possessed* is not only an honor to many literary women; it's an image of death as something more beautiful than it is—a death beyond death, its redemption.

— CHARLENE ELSBY, AUTHOR OF
PSYCHROS & *HEXIS*

The "little death" of orgasm isn't so small after all in Adrian Ernesto Cepeda's *We Are the Ones Possessed*. With the historical awareness of a cento and the contemporality of a soundbite, Cepeda explores the knotted entanglement of poetry's two age-old obsessions--sex and death-- with an eye toward tying the knot tighter rather than separating terror from pleasure. "Waiting under the mistletoe with a knife," this book rubs romance against bare mortality until the two fuse inextricably--a marriage too often relegated to the realms of erotica and gore. Cepeda reminds us, such a union is the home of poets, where horror and desire cuddle up together, swap spit, and let the boundary between them blur.

— DYLAN KRIEGER, AUTHOR OF
SOFT

Adrian Ernesto Cepeda's poems always leave me breathless; *We Are the Ones Possessed* is no different. The lines can be mistakenly simple but say so much—like watching snow fall over a lake. Lines like "I suggest we roll down/the windows, reverse/our front seat" create gorgeous images while also narrating the mundane yet poignant moments in our lives. This book tells us how we possess ourselves and others—and how no one gets away unscathed.

— JOANNA C. VALENTE, AUTHOR OF *A LOVE STORY, NO(BODY), SEXTING GHOSTS,* AND *SIRS & MADAMS*

Haunting, unnerving and sexy, Adrian Ernesto Cepeda's *We Are the Ones Possessed* makes a case for dark poetry with his collection of passionate calamities, smearing his poems with feverish pleasures, cursed confessions and death shadows lusting for Blood.

— JEAN-PIERRE RUEDA, AUTHOR OF *HERENCIAS* FROM ALEGRÍA PUBLISHING

Few poets know sex and death as well as Adrian Ernesto Cepeda, whose verse relishes in the escape, release, and transformation that both pleasure and the cessation of life have to offer. Each piece in *We Are the Ones Possessed* is a petite mort—a potent and intoxicating little death that scares us titillated—and through these poems we may learn how to live and die deliciously.

— KIM VODICKA, AUTHOR OF *DEAR TED* AND *THE ELVIS MACHINE*

We Are the Ones Possessed marries the corporeal horror of a Cronenberg film with the gauzy, creeping uneasiness of a midnight ghost tour in Salem, Massachusetts. A must read for fans of the ethereal and sublime.

— KOLLEEN CARNEY HOEPFNER, EIC, *DRUNK MONKEY*

Spellbinding, sensual, and sinister, Cepeda's *We Are the Ones Possessed* is a powerhouse collection of sex & death that excites the senses with every line. This is wedding-in-a-graveyard poetry. This is strip-naked-&-worship-the-moon poetry. This is wash-down-your-ex's-heart-with-champagne poetry. Decadent, deadly, & as consumptive as *Possessed* is compelling.

— JESSICA MCHUGH, BRAM STOKER AWARD NOMINATED AUTHOR OF *A COMPLEX ACCIDENT OF LIFE*

With nods to various icons of art, music, and literature, these pieces are so beautiful and stunning. Gilded in twilight and darkness, *We Are the Ones Possessed* is a collection of poetry that guides us along fragments of moments, with the tortured and the torturer. Scenes in dark rooms, across environments and situations pulsate with bloody ecstasy, attraction, and betrayal. *We Are the Ones Possessed* shows us not only what we've had done to us, but what we have done.

— CYNTHIA PELAYO, BRAM STOKER AWARD NOMINATED AUTHOR OF *CHILDREN OF CHICAGO*

We Are the Ones Possessed is a vivid, heart breaking, and tragic collection of poems that drips from the pages with the viscosity of blood. Cepeda is a Latinx talent you should be reading as a horror and poetry fan. I highly recommend this beautiful book that reaches out and grabs you by the heart and throat. I adored *Night Stalker Tattoo on Her Back*.

— V. CASTRO, AUTHOR OF *THE QUEEN OF THE CICADAS*

Cepeda's haunting poems, inspired by existing written work and visuals, are a medley of daydreams & nightmares, floating in the middle of a fateful dance of death and sex. The winged beauty in the shadows of love/revenge painted by his exceptional verse in *We Are the Ones Possessed* will take your breath away.

— LINDA D. ADDISON, AWARD-WINNING AUTHOR, HWA LIFETIME ACHIEVEMENT AWARD RECIPIENT AND SFPA GRAND MASTER

We Are the Ones Possessed brings poems that read like a movie you just don't want to end. Cepeda's brand of horror opens portals into worlds, immersing you into a collection of work that will leave you wondering if there's anything more horrific than the human condition itself, and his brand of poetry is like breath of fresh winter air — addictive and piercing. Cepeda's work will sink its teeth into you and play on loop in your subconscious for years to come. A beautifully haunting piece of art.

— JEAN-MARIE BUB, AUTHOR OF *MANEATER*

WE ARE THE ONES POSSESSED

31 poems that end the same

ADRIAN ERNESTO CEPEDA

CL◢SH

"Death must be so beautiful"

Sylvia Plath

FOREWORD

I know *We Are the Ones Possessed* is not your traditional idea of horror. I wanted to face Death as a theme that has haunted my imagination for 50 years.

The idea for *La Petite Mort* came to me while listening to Nick Cave and The Bad Seeds' *Murder Ballads* and reading Carmen Maria Machado's beautiful chilling *Her Body and Other Parties*.

I believe the poems in this collection resonate a little death as these verses will shock and unnerve while lingering with you long after you reach the fatal conclusion of: *We Are the Ones Possessed*.

Thank You also to Sadie, Ashley of Night Worms for their support and inspiration in this personal poetry project that is *We Are the Ones Possessed*.

"More Than an Accessory" appears in *Written Tales*

CONTENTS

INTRODUCTION
BY
SADIE HARTMANN

✦

In July 2020 my business partner Ashley and I curated a package for our horror subscription service, Night Worms. We celebrated Latinx writers including two books, *MEXICAN GOTHIC* a Gothic horror novel by Silvia Moreno-Garcia, and *LA BELLE AJAR* by Adrian Ernesto Cepeda- a collection of cento poems inspired by Silvia Plath's *THE BELL JAR*. My business partner, Ashley Saywers is a big fan of Silvia Plath so as soon as she heard of Cepeda's new CLASH books release, she championed the idea of sending it out to horror fans through Night Worms. Her plan worked! **LA BELLE AJAR** was embraced openly by our customers.

✦

I enjoyed **LA BELL AJAR** too but I write this introduction with a posture of humility. My love of poetry is brand new. Adrian Ernesto Cepeda graciously honors me with his invitation to write the foreword to **WE ARE THE ONES POSSESSED**. I feel like someone who is learning how to swim. Sometimes I venture into a poetry collection and the waters are too deep for me; I'm not confident in the strokes. Other times, everything feels just right. I'm the most at home with horror fiction. It's my comfort zone. My happy place. A few years ago, I discovered there are poets out there writing about death, human monsters, possession, and other macabre subjects. I've been a fan of "dark poetry" ever since this remarkable discovery.

Specifically, I respond to Adrian's style and voice as well as the textures of a quilted, patchwork poem, known as cento poetry. **WE ARE THE ONES POSSESSED** is a balance of both cento and traditional form poetry.

"A cento poem is a work of poetry that is composed of various lines taken from different poems. The word "cento" is derived from a Latin word meaning "patchwork garment"—and a cento poem is just that— patchwork poetry."--Masterclass.com

❧

The Cento poem breathes life into *We are the Ones*, a collection of death poems. The essence and spirit of *Murder Ballads* lives Possessed within each verse leading you deeper into the darkness and holding you captive to every page.
This opportunity to take your arm under mine and walk with you into **WE ARE THE ONES POSSESSED** gives us a unique kinship. But we are already unified by these two subjects:
Death and Sex.

The poems in this collection marry these two subjects together in an intoxicating and alluring union. One minute, you're absorbed by the entanglement of two bodies in a dirty, public bathroom. The next, sexy wordplay. In fact, this is one of Adrian's signature moves-taking ordinary objects or tasks (driving the car,

shooting a gun, eating breakfast) and sexing it up! (for
lack of better words)
Death and Sex.

Are there any other topics as universal or relatable?

WE ARE THE ONES POSSESSED.

I hope you enjoy your journey.
Sadie Hartmann "Mother Horror"
January 6th, 2021

FURIOUS AND DRUNK

*Cento poem from Dream House as House in Iowa section in
Carmen Maria Machado's 2020 book*

you follow watching
her tinfoil head angry
conspiracy stumbling
to anger— like before,
a wasted ghost, face
widening snarl force
a terrible touch, you
tell her grasp *fuck
you.* kicking knobs
then yelling inside, she
jumps to scare you into
a scream, *you fucked this
night.* drunken this time
the villain she scorns and
slams, your body slices—
your weeping chest begins

falling ahead the mirror
fills with a smoky seared
angel, she stalks the blankest
angry eye dead-darker
stared feed past creamily
emerging patches of skin
yelling *fuck* — you almost
lived. she snaps, your
girlfriend cuts you into
heavenly bits, draping
pieces into torso blue,
you underestimated her
hands. Confused, you
dye watching texture
life fumes soundlessly
swirling down the drain.

SHE DELETED MY CONTACT
FROM HER IPHONE 6

Ana loved leaving me
breathless always in the
Le Bon Temps Roule stall,
although I worked the late
shift with her bartender
girlfriend, the only place
she would rendezvous
with me was in this filthy
washroom. Despite the steam
whispering she loved the flavor
of my violet grape lipstick,
everything still hazy inside
my head, I recall how she
loved me submissively
heaving, already knowing
my inhaler was in my black
purse on the bar. I remember
while clutching my heels,
Ana grinded above
my short waitress skirt,
seeing her holding on to the

gray graffiti walls, calling
me, her *dirty damsel*, shoving
her inked beautifully
tattooed tit # 13 through
her red lacy top all over
my face, knowing, I could
never resist her lusciously
suffocating me, Unable to
breathe, devouring every
inch of me, she perky
excited as this Lazarus lady
whispers *I am I am I am*
your last, baby — when
the lights faded out, a little
death came over splashing
me realizing as horns from
a New Orleans jazz funky
funeral passed me on Rampart
St. reminding me of the Zulu
Parade on Mardi Gras, but
this time as my grandmother's
gold bracelets jangled
and jingled, I could feel
my coffin floating in
rhythm more than just
corazon stabbing pain
in my bustier chest,
I had the scars to prove
my fate, above the drums
and cacophony of horns,
wondering would anyone
catch my screams —
so much darkness, all I
could faintly overhear
was her sadistic cackling

while picturing Ana flashing
her magnificently tattooed
chest. I could tell by the
drunk tone of my dominating
lover she was already
searching for the next femme
to prey. Never questioning,
why she could not resist
swallowing the drink
spiked Ana gave me, numbing
me paralyzed, sweetened
with her poisonous aftertaste —
cotton mouth haunts me, along
with the holes in the coffin,
daylight peaking everything
a blur while still thirsting
this hangover, I could
barely see over my fake
lashes. Inside this casket,
as each shoveled earth
lands like dirt waves
crashing all over
my uptown grave
I can feel the night
worms crawling through
my Tipitina's crop top —
chewing mind bites
beyond these hair
extensions inside my
frizzy comatose head —
gasping, if I am history,
have I already passed?

A GHOST CAN BE A LOT OF THINGS[1]

A daydream memory,
secret guilt, most times,
in grief, we wish to see
a ghost[2]. Loss, an emotion
of love, or blood, hold us
to a time, they remain a
place, a drive those like
a crime, conscience speaking
to the dead[3], never go away[4]
alive we carry ghosts people
inside us[5] uttering, broken
yourself the same lonely[6]
spirit, demon, look[7]
keep them[8] cuts, and skin
happening to you, pain
opens whispering hell
in this head look[9], ghosts
as memory unconscious[10],
the sound of footsteps we
call them[11] a memory
repressed the present
demanding a ghost in
the past.[12] My soul cannot
live[13] tonight fear was
haunted this night[14] without
ghosts, take me, rest not,
I am, mad, Oh God, take
me, haunt my life. I believe
in this abyss I am living[15],
shadow[16] dark, beneath,

move between dust unseen[17]
come back as a dream[18].
Past, future, present scares
yet[19] I believe, ourselves,
we haunt[20] nothing more
than ghosts living[21] to ache
torment to appear unwanted[22]
they were haunting[23], alive,
you should try to hear the dead,
the cries[24], death dwells in
eternal darkness,[25] uninvited
ghosts[26], keep on haunting
me, begging[27], to haunt
you,[28] does the dark burn?[29]
The dying speak in the circle
of the room,[30] looking sadly
through the window[31] you
won't turn away.[32] let in
the tension especially when
held between the being, you
can't let go[33], the grimace
lain, the fleshless body
looking down[34], Your smell,
how is this dead?[35]

1. *The Haunting of Hill House* (2018) dir. Mike Flanagan
2. *The Haunting of Hill House* (2018) dir. Mike Flanagan
3. **Jim Carroll**
4. *Crimson Peak* (2015) dir. Guillermo del Toro
5. **Liam Callanan**, *The Cloud Atlas*
6. **George Orwell**, *1984*
7. **Leanna Renee Hieber**, *The Strangely Beautiful Tale of Miss Percy Parker*
8. **Rob Montgomery**
9. **Emily Andrews**, *The Finer Points of Becoming Machine*
10. **Emily Andrews**, *The Finer Points of Becoming Machine*
11. **Donna Tartt**, *The Secret History*

12. **Alfred Mac Adam**, Introduction of Jane Austen's *Northanger Abbey*
13. **Emily Brontë**, *Wuthering Heights*
14. **John Steinbeck**, *Tortilla Flat*
15. **Emily Brontë**, *Wuthering Heights*
16. **Euripides**, *Herakles*
17. **Neil Gaiman**, *The Graveyard Book*
18. **Euripides**, *Herakles*
19. **Lidia Longorio**, *Hey Humanity*
20. **Laurie Halse Anderson**, *Wintergirls*
21. **Libba Bray**, *A Great and Terrible Beauty*
22. **Randon Billings Noble**, *Be with Me Always: Essays*
23. **Libba Bray**, *A Great and Terrible Beauty*
24. **Philip K. Dick**, *VALIS*
25. D.L. Lewis
26. **Stephen King**, *Bag of Bones*
27. **Haunting**, *Halsey*
28. **Haunt**, *Bastille*
29. **D.M. Siciliano**, *Inside*
30. **Susanna Moore**, *In the Cut*
31. **Anthony Horowitz**, *Magpie Murders*
32. **Randon Billings Noble**, *Be with Me Always: Essays*
33. **Randon Billings Noble**, *Be with Me Always: Essays*
34. **William Faulkner**, *A Rose for Emily*
35. **Valzhyna Mort**, *Factory of Tears*

HER GARAGE EMOTES

Unexplained, seductive, never detained, never enough.
— Anne Sexton

I can tell turning
the key ignition,
smoky like a daydream
fogging windows, without
nicotine, leaning over
turned on already
with exhaust on our lips,
our tongues the ink
licking like pens
no paper necessary
with our climactic kiss,
Anne wants to make
out with poems,
in between breaths
I suggest we roll down
the windows, reverse

our front seat getaway
I can feel the driveway
still exist, but she just
wants to park, her tongue
in my mouth, imagining
our cul-de-sac getaway
Sexton's foot on the gas
wanting this climax
to last, with our littlest
death, she whispers
we are eternal, wanting
me to take the wheel,
wanting to feel me driving
deeper forgetting horizons
she loves restarting me
with a spark, she exhales —
lover divine me as we
exhaust on last eclipsing
breaths hazy $Co2$ clouds
engulf us, more than one
final kiss, Anne loves idling
eternally inside my mouth.

THE SPACE BETWEEN

You love to find me
below you Your body,
a temple I worship you
towering above me gasping
at your glorious terrain.
Grinding loving my tongue
exploring so many shades,
colors blushing before me
more than paints all that's left
on these bedsheets are sweet
drips of sweat, chalk outlines
me dying for more, feeling
captured while enrapturing me
devouring kisses, as you
spread teasing my mouth
loving to swallow every after
taste of my last breath, loving
to see me so beautiful barely
awakened as I fade, your
lips softly smothering any
exhales, so blue, my body
stiffening eternally my face
remains asphyxiating between
flatlines of unconsciousness.

ASSIA'S FEET ALMOST
TOUCHED THE DOOR

Barely conscious her last
Thought of Ted Hughes'
first wife, she could never
replace, so she joined Sylvia
Plath instead, on the other
side of the stove. Assia
switched off, swallowing
so many sleeping pills,
hoping one last swig from
the whiskey bottle would
conjure the happy ending
dream that always eluded
her. She envied of the leaking
gas that oozed for Sivvy, now
that they are the same, fatally
estranged Assia finally envisions
a place the three of them can be
together, but before Wevill
could make it through towards
the cloudy light, as her feet
almost touching the door

to the other side, cracked
opening, no more Ted, as she
enters holding her little daughter's
hand, the first hazy soul she
encounters seeing Sylvia waving
back, *no longer the mistress,*
I am mother she kept telling
herself, instead, even in this
afterlife, Assia tired of being
in Plath's shadow, alas…
hearing this invincible laugh
as this American poet
mouths: *finally…*

                    —- *you're dead.*

NIGHT STALKER TATTOO ON
HER BACK

He speaks to Carrie cackling
instructions *keep sharpening
your knife*, in the dark,
alone with so many of
his headlines, profiles,
headshots on her white
walls, picturing his blood
scattering like an unfinished
canvas on her wall, each
blade is her paintbrush as
she converses nightly with
this imprisoned serial killer,
Richard Ramirez, from Carrie's
NOLA apartment on Royal
Street, Night Stalker sends
her letters of suggestions
others blood is our sustenance
she memorizes and when
sleeping starkly, Carrie uses
his words as covers, blanketing
with so many ideas on how

to hunt and slay a stranger
which she uses stalking
the French Quarter in her
highest of heels, tight short
skirts and even lower white
neckline tee, so the blood can
splash on her shirt, Carrie follows
Ramirez voice always in her head,
time to go hunting so she starts by
taking shots at Maple Leaf Bar,
pub crawling trying to size up
the perfect one at a dive bar
on Decatur, instantly making
contact. She eyes on her
prey, long hair, puppy dog
looks, shirt open showing
chest hair the Night Stalker
speaks *Yes!* approving of Carrie's
choice that is ready to be trimmed
bare by her blade, their gaze
meet, sharing drinks, she shoots
daggers of flirtation trying to
mesmerize this stranger for one
last night rendezvous —*make
the first move*, The Night Stalker
whispers as she points leading
him outside, Carrie follows, with
each heel echoing step, she desires
to feel his flesh slashed. When
they reach his loft, Richard commands
show him my face, so she peels off
her top, turns around showing
him her skin art tribute, Night
Stalker tattoo covering all of her
back, as Carrie lies ready on his bed,

clutching the knife, this stranger
switches off the red light, sliding
in bed, ready to be the victim
she lusts to turn him sliced, gasping
bloodthirsty, Carrie hungers to
slaughter, she begins to cut. *Again!*
Ramirez demands, following each
stabbing order, thanking her Richard,
her savior of slaughter as her stranger
slumps over covered in lethal slashes—
Your first masterpiece! Ramirez praises,
encouraging Carrie to *Slice Deeper*!
Longing for more, she finishes with
a long red kiss, wanting to taste his
breathless lips, swallowing
his last screams, Richard gleams
so deadly, you're a Natural! As
Carrie seductively slays on red sheets,
The Night Stalker continuously seduces
her ear, *with his cuts you become immortal*—
grinning in puddles Carrie is ready
to follow Richard's hypnotic lead,
after quickly acquiring the taste,
she is eager to explore by stabbing
the bloody remains for so many more.

WAITING UNDER THE MISTLETOE WITH A KNIFE IN MY HAND

"She does not know how to shiver. She has her knife and she is afraid of nothing."

— *Angela Carter, The Bloody Chamber*

From the window, day
dreaming I can hear
my indiscreet husband
stumbling up the driveway,
as I stand waiting inside
under the mistletoe, in
my hand the knife, tired
of being gaslit behind
the stove, although
he wishes I would stick
my head inside, no,
instead, I grip cutting
board fantasies ready
to see his bleeding

pleas as he begs for
his life so worthless,
every wife disgusted
and jilted desires
to play my role
the widow grieving
tears that crocodile
under my veil, ready
under the mistletoe
with a knife in my hand,
forget yoga— I am
premediating when he
staggers in for the last
time, seeing the doorknob
turn, I can already taste
his final drunken breaths
fantasizing of gift wrap
his bloody leftovers,
his stench I will not miss
from all his holiday office
parties so many secretaries
perfume and lipstick
neck now eternally slashed
and stained, his remains
wrapped in the imported
carpet, even when shaving
he bleeds so much,
memorizing my lines
I rehearse for the fuzz,
the mourning wife
teary red champagned
eyed from staying up,
now I am the one with
the buzz this day I seized,
under the mistletoe with

a knife in my hand, no
more retorts with each cut
watching him gush with
sangre, already I will no
long Mrs. the perishing
breaths of this
promiscuous sleaze.

Thank You Lindsay Lerman

I AM 8,000 NERVE FIBERS

When aiming for me,
please remember to
be precise; I am
more than just for
cock and reloading —
forget your cross, I am
pure on purpose,
there's a higher
concentration hiding
well-deserved desires.
I know you long firing
everywhere else, the rounds
you love spraying all over
this voluptuous frame. Target
if you can find me with practice,
please pray while trying
to worship me on your knees,
speaking secret alphabets
with lips, using tongue
and your fingertips

that's a better clip
than twice the number
in your biggest barrel.
Remember try not
triggering me erratic.
please give it twice or
moreover, and over, slowly,
more than practice, patience
is the most perfect piece —
try gunning for my release
by atoning for your friendly
fire. Your chamber empties
already? Think beyond
the feel of your metal heart.
Unsatisfying shooter, you
missed again? Tired of you
already reaching for her favorite
weapon. Round after round
will leave a splatter of bloody
ecstasy stains, your corpse
rotten deadweight all over
her bedsheets. did you forget
when you met at the gun
range that she wouldn't
emptying every chamber,

sorry darling, she no longer
needs nor desires your puny
little pistol. Licking the end
of her gun, she lives for
muzzling your last muffled
screams, as this fatale femme
stands over your carcass, more
than just blowing smoke, while

coming over your chalk outline,
your favorite bang mouths:
like my favorite vibrator —
I grip semi-automatic.

Thank You Natalie Angier

SHE EATS MEN FOR BREAKFAST

From a photograph of Sylvia Plath at Mademoiselle, 1953

She lives for forking
each one, proudly
prickling eggs watching
their yokes cum
all over her plate. She
loves chewing on
their limp shells, crunching
on their bacon limbs,
nibbling on their body
of toast. As she spreads
jelly ready to jam
their melting buttery
relations with the saltiest
after taste, deep
inside. Sometimes,
adding pepper for the sunny
side mouthful sensations,

she loves swallowing
their simmering links.
Using teeth, it's the only
morning after bed
and breakfast meal
that satisfies her carnal
cravings. Forget blowing
steam from whip cream
clouds in her AM coffee,
she loves spooning
with the cold leftovers
remaining wet while
reheating desires, nakedly
she loves dangling
their dingleberries
over her tongue,
she always sizzles
for this lusty flame
all morning hungering
she remains sticky
stained syrupy for one
final spoonful, feasting
on his ribs, satiating
every flavorful limb
for breakfast, leaves her
so unsatisfied.

YOU ARE THE ONES
POSSESSED

*From Nicolas Francois Octave Tassaert's painting La Femme
Damnée (The Cursed Woman), 1859*

Pleasure givers, the way
you have your mouths
on both lips and her chest,
she is the one still floating
skyward and you are the ones
trying to bring her down but
instead these licks gifting
more desire keeps lifting her
higher with the divinest
of drips, all that you savor
the holiest drops, this goddess
ruler of our universe, this
and every planet becomes
more powerful, no mortal
man can ignore her desire
when she comes you are

the one being drained, loving
her climatic refrains she is
the goddess her thunder
resounds on every blow,
as she bellows loudly this
firess who loves sparking
the flame as she soars
empowering, your licks
becoming energetic of riches,
although it looks like
she is being swayed
by your temptation but
foolish boys, although she
glows naked it is clear
from this rendezvous,
this goddesses body reining
proudly above the obsessive
three are the ones unable to stop
awarding earth shattering
climaxes, breathless
lips have nothing more to
give, revealing a death little
more than just possessed —
she is the one cursing you.

DESIRE MUERTE

From Edvard Munch's Death of Marat I, Oil on canvas, 1907.

Especially as I lie
casket like beside
you, feel your body
in the dark cloaking
me while in my blindfold
imagining flashes of
our attractions coming
in between feel you
my pale rider, hands
on my throat, capturing
each excited exhale by
hypnotically restricting
passageways, flicking
light, feeling gates, pearls
around my neck and then
darkness returns, you live
for tempting me, with

each command seeing
me restrained my palpitating
heart stops and restarts
teasing my second coming,
almost reaching my climax,
one final glimpse, angels,
demons surrounding
along with your naked
cackles, before collapsing
hear you licking lips whisper
not this time, while untying
me, leaving me sticky, whip
stained bloody scars, each
faint blink gives me a taste
wanting to savor more than
a little death, leaving me
unsatisfied, coffin craving
never fearing the last sound,
I will hear, as you my angel
exhume's my final falsetto,
desiring next time my dominate
undertaker will allow muerte
to swallow me leaving nothing
but my erected headstone.

SHE WRITHES OF FIRE

"… the irrepressible tremulous light in her eyes and smile burned him"

— *Leo Tolstoy*

All over ablaze
so beautifully
illuminating like a nebula
star expanding in the dark,
above me I can feel universes
expanding as she swallows
me, rekindle her like fuel
as gasoline odors ooze
I feel her flames under
my skin it's like someone
lit a match
and there's a fire burning
up and down my arms,
I can feel the pitchforks

scorching my flesh,
I've got the devil in me,
and she wants to cause
burns third degrees
leave me flaming,
wildfire on my knees.
All I wanted was one more
hit, I've got the devil
in me striking the match
inhaling my favorite green,
but with every joint, bong
rip, vape the smoke causes
more blazing on my body,
curled up in a fireball
no water can put this
inferno out. My addiction
rekindles this blaze I've got
the devil in me, all over
my torso, all though
looking down my skin
is fine, underneath
no longer pink, I've got
the devil in me, I can
feel my insides scorching
for the one reignites
my dependence, the devil
has a name, my flesh
craving her pitchforks
scarring under my skin,
so, obsessed she owns
every inch, my body
torches eternally enflamed
I can feel her inhale while
she incinerates me

FURTHER I WILL NOT
VENTURE ALONE

From Maanantai Collective 2013 pigment print framed

I am tired of the cold,
the shivering chills
the constant washing
and rewashing
of my hands, some
days I don't recognize
my once familiar finger
prints, now eternally pruned
from sanitizing of hands,
soap foaming antibacterial,
I just want my hands to
caresses and touch all
the imperfect wrinkles
from my now untouchable
face. I cover up with masks
so surgical, every time
even when a finger grazes a

surface, countertop or
cardboard shipping box
foreign, I must scrub
my palms scalding water
always hot, I can no longer
enjoy shopping, why must
customers hoard all the rolls
of Charmin toilet paper,
jugs of water, all the shelves
in my local stories, once
Wal Mart now Target
is empty, pushing carts
gripping with rubber gloves
why does it feel like we
are already living in
a wasteland, breathing
corpses afraid of breathing,
shaking hands, hugging
each other, as I follow
my husband to our car
overstuffed with end
of the world, Apocalypse
groceries, I just want
to rush home on the now
empty streets, my after
dinner look already signals
you to drop the bags
on the too clean table
and strip down to nothing
and feel our bodies skin
on skin, leaving the window
cracked as the cold wind
shivers our flesh, eyes rolls
why did we leave our masks
off while mocking the fear

that surrounded us on every
channel? All TV news fake,
we broadcast our own feed
watching me touching no
longer, so many scabs pussing
proudly on your cheeks on
the filthy kitchen floor
starving to explore, we can
hear the angels calling us
breaths gasp for one final
kiss, but we lie on tiles
between us so many vows
left unfulfilled, feeling us
drifting off together, our faces
quiver while death cackles
all over— dying for a taste
of your every pore.

I COULDN'T DEAL WITH THE LARGE PARTS YET

Cento Poem from Charlene Elsby's Hexis

Picking little flesh bits
away relentless skin
the senses here trying to
hair drain my intention
down, small nail bits
anything to visibly
speed up the diluting skin,
death remained a scent
of ruined bleach body,
unwanted spread bleach
ruined the bathroom, bleach
smell in the bathtub was
heavy, the surface bleach
air hit me terrible, downward
I would sink to the floor and
drip lower than the bones

in the toilet. My problem,
the farther I reached
the same confining
hands of my hell —
always would drain me.

"I JUST NEED A RENDEZVOUS FOR BREAKFAST."

Cento Poem from Lindsay Lerman's I'm From Nowhere

Following desire, she
likes to see Andrew
hard, he turns pleasure
snaking wanted fire,
his fingers tear clothing,
she slaps his breath, her
teeth land behind his back,
she bites, catches blood,
his mouth thirsty small,
possessively hungry she
likes loudly drinking his
reflexive body, underneath
legs emphasizing touching,
her need to be wrapped
around Andrew, tightly
they fuck against
the uncomfortable café

wall. Familiar and tired
her intensity wishes, he
would be finished. Andrew
needs to surrender on his
simple knees. Her libido
takes to eat him whole.
She says don't come.
Her mouth talking close
to his ear. *Ready. They
both know what's coming
next.* On top, smothering
Andrew's face, with his last
gasp, she wants her period
so… he can taste her blood.

CAN YOU HANDLE "THE FLESH" IN THE CRONENBERG SENSE?

Are you ready to feel
the ooze all over your
body, the tentacles
of creatures biting
love nibbles, chewing
your skin, you must
love the creature transforming
inside of me, do you
want to feel my teeth,
ready for the bloody
to spray out all over
so much desire spewing
all over with so many
sounds, aromas, cravings
spreading excited excretions
that I long for you to savor
each flavor seeping out
my bed becomes necropolis
for hungry, for those of you
starving for more than my flesh
craving to carve each layer

are you ready to stretch
my cartilage licking up
the gushing arousal
plasma serum, while you
clench my neck, gorging on
every Riga-mortis aftertaste —
will you beg me to more
than suck while facing
the climaxing gluttony
dying to gasp your
little last breath.

Thank You Dylan Krieger

DEATH PORTRAITS

No need for this family
member to glare into
the brightness, by painting
pupils of this memento mori
keepsake within 24 hours of
postmortem, this morbid
darkroom Victorian sensation
is anything but morbid as
the very shadowy photograph
of a loved one is fixed forever
by adding silver polish, this
shade of tint brings heavenly
calm into their departed
cheeks. Each daguerreotype
frame blurs the sharpness
of grief as each camera gleams
to portrait a body once breathing,
his spirit already floating into
the next light. With each flash,
everyone smells the same,
the gaze of the camera makes

each subject mortal, no
longer rich, this state
of mortuary captures
the same pale pulseless
skin. One final pose as
this suited up cadaver now
casket ready, just like
the others, with every
smokey snapshot —
he lifelessly leans towards
the other side.

WHAT DOES LAURA SEE?

I hear your voice and see your shadow
— Anna Margolin

Does she picture her
future? Screaming Bob,
flashing forward
plastic bags, rivers icy
wrapped in seaweed,
filthy waters stained
in flesh of the innocent—
everyone is guilty
in this town. Every one
eyed jack wanted to
go all in with her,
every Double R. Diner
girl wanted a beau like
hers, every Great Northern
woman loathed the sight
of her, still, everywhere

she went every eye in Twin
Peaks loved to gossip while
ogling, if even for an instant—
while fatale femme Laura
glows behind the lens, does
she pictures her future
Leland's weeping as the camera
focuses on scarlet "r" found
under her fingernails, scratching
evidence from beyond,
Agent Cooper tape recording
clues by the water
before the fade out her
light once floating now waves
will also come Falling from
a glimpse of her eye, Laura's
skies shivering already from
the video clips you can tell
Miss Palmer loved soaking
in eternity.

"LITTLE LATE TODAY, FOLKS"

The lottery dances
round, as the sorry
square villagers murmur
beamed a stone drawing
desperately for conversations
distance, blank space
removed hesitation, inside
the original lottery old
born upset tradition,
every box constructed
new ritual forgotten,
successful population
growing, box lottery
was made of paper taken
into the box. Sometimes
it spent a year fussing,
the lottery declared
lists of families, each
family members
remembered as the chant

rattled this tuneless ritual
sang, the kids left gone,
addressing a proper
salute to the box. Villagers
hurriedly assembled, time
clearly forget what dried
day, time still was talking
Mrs., found her Hutchinson
children and husband though
the farewell crowd. Get this
started. Boy tall Watson
drawing old expression
here, hush sudden look
as Summers voice cleared,
ready, take names out of
quiet box. Paper folded
families apart as time
greeted lotteries forward —
next all the men nervously
holding papers in their crazy
hands. Folks young wanting
to quit lotteries, as everybody
stewed together, pack of
precisely trouble fools, hurry
take the slip from the lottery
box. Suddenly, the paper opened
a pause long and breathless,
Hutchinson paper began voices,
to say and speak, staring all
Summers snapped the slip
the sound of the box whispered
a blank sigh, quickly the ritual
forgotten the box black, the stones
said hurry, the crowd moved

large, as the graves hit upon
her little scraps of head.

Cento poem from Shirley Jackson's 1948 short story

I STILL REMEMBER THE
SCENT OF HER APARTMENT

"What's more romantic than
Dying in the moonlight"

— *Tom Waits*

When we walked in with
the gurney, the aroma of
burned out Nag Champa
in the air, seeing her on the
hardwood floor, copy of
Her Body and Other Parties
next to the nightstand along
with stacks of Bad Seed CD's,
some of my favorites. She
looked pale, shoulder length
brown hair, wearing a scissor
V cut black *The Bell Jar* tee,
the original cover Plath used

Victoria Lucas as her pen
name. Immediately I could
tell this was far from being
another 9-11 call. As I leaned
in to see if she was breathing
I caught a whiff of her sweet
exhale, reminding me of
Hawaiian Punch and Pirate
Morgan drinks I would mix
for my friends. When my
fingers touched her cheek
I felt a very faint pulse, yet
also, an instant spark. *She
needs mouth to mouth*, my
EMT partner yelled out.
I started chest compressions,
while placing my lips on
hers—it was like a detonation.
She was soft, sweet, like
we had kissed. But she
was not breathing. I tried
over and over, blowing
exhales inside her lungs
but nothing. There was little
life left inside her. But I
couldn't stop, I kept trying
to resuscitate her. This was
more just than another distress call
this was fate. But, even as
they took her body away
to the morgue, it was not
over for me. The remnants
of our first the aftertaste
our last kiss, lingered
inside me. With every call

I silently hoped, we would
find her again, on the floor,
and this time I could save
her, but not, each night
that passed, sitting inside
the ambulance it's like
a part of me had passed and
her presence was living
inside my lips, my mind
could not stop reliving
the night we almost met,
how could this girl who
could have been my one
no longer exist? In my
apartment after an all
nighter, I sit with a bottle
of pills, taking them out
one by one, ready to
take each one, it was
as if my life was before
and after the girl with
Victoria Lucas shirt, when
her lips kissed mine, I was
a frog and now her good
night prince was ready to
fly. Believe me, I tried
drowning out her taste,
so many whiskeys, vodka,
gin shots but I could still
taste her presence inside
my mouth, some at work
called her my addiction,
like her, I was ready to
to talk like angels, emptying
these pills, one by one, as I

wait for my siren, I can
almost feel her lips —
I know the EMT's would
ask why? For her I would
swallow everything.

HER FAVORITE ID CHANNEL SHOW ALWAYS REFLECTING MY NAME

Wishing I had a royal taster
when I take bites from her
every meal, wondering is
there is a special killer seasoning
inside this dish? Am I the only
husband whose wife is obsessed
with murder shows? Every time
I hear the *Your Worst Nightmar*e
theme, I swear she is ID channeling
always taking mental white out
notes on how to expertly dispose
of my lanky lazy boy body...
is she planning *A Crime to Remember*
or is it all in my head, the way
she is always reading about Jodi
Arias, it feels like her eyes are
knives sharpening their *20/20*
focus on me. It makes me second
guess should we go on our scuba
diving vacation, will I be the only one
who makes it back alive? Should

I be worried that she is always
blasting every *48 Hours*, *Forensic
Files*, I don't want to be a *Cold
Case*, mystery unsolved, before
I try to drift off some nights, I
swear I imagine hearing Keith
Morrison narrating my future
Homicide already preordained.
If I do not wake up will *the LA
Times* print my obituary with
my penname? Should I lie
awake so I don't miss my demise
to be televised on a two part
Dateline NBC exclusive,
our neighbors interviewed
saying how they never over
heard the muted poetic howls
of my last prophetic refrain.

MORE THAN AN ACCESSORY

Cento poem from Carmen Maria Machado's *Her Body and Other Parties*

I am her ribbon, the one
she keeps around her long
swan like neck of her body
and the envy of the other
luscious parts. I come in
red, her favorite color, I
never stray from her collar
line, even when her husbands
hands become so frisky trying
to loosen every strap, he tries
to untie me when he smoothly
whispers how much he loves
her face, uses words like
perfection and model, but
she always slaps him away.
He refuses to accept, she

and I are united forever,
his wife is more faithful
to me than she is loyal to his
two-minute orgasms. I love
the feel of being attached to her
gullet, I can feel her when
she snored counting sheep
while fantasy dreaming,
swallowing the creamiest
shakes even when she
has a cold, every phlegm
that flies out of her throat
I can feel it pulse through me.
then one night, I could tell
something was rotten as her
husband enticed her to play
a kinky game. He wanted to
tie her up, I worried about
his intensions, still I remained
convinced he would leave his
dirty hands off me, but then,
I felt his fingers loosen me
from her neck, this is when
he carried me from their
bed, I felt the scissors. Before
the first cut, we both turned
hearing something round
cranium-like fall on
the floor, this is when
I felt each snip, *off with your
head*. Why did he have to be
so vain? I was the auricular
nerve that held her up. As
I lay shattered barely alive,
I watched him pathetically

trying to put his wife back
together, like a doll in pieces,
she no longer was the most
perfect face, the one he longed
to keep mantled his trophy
wife now becomes a torso,
blood rushing out of her
thyroid glands, no longer
attached, he never wanted
to see that I was the bow on
his gift that kept her trachea
bonded. He should have never
been fixated on severing my hold.
What happened to the vows?
now he must have been witholding
this body without his favorite part.

LAS VEGAS STRIP: SEPT 7, 1996

Knight's BMW stalled
11:15 PM Flamingo
and Kovel riddled with
plethora of silver bullet
holes. Scent of gun
fire burns the sweat tinged
of an entourages confusion
muggy midnight air. As
Vegas peace officer opens
the passenger side door to
see this non-apologetic
revolutionary who was able
to take a stand against the
5-0 all draped in black,
his dark skin glowing
under the streetlights flushed
like a King; Gold necklace
and jewelry gushing Mob
Piru Bloods. Falling out
of the door, now laying
on Vegas pavement. Breathing

sporadically, gurgling last
breaths his concrete
consciousness slipping
never gripping fear as death's
angel stood so near. Hearing
the last beats coming, scratching
closer, uncensored till the end
bold, unapologetic, abrasive,
intimidating. His present alone
was like a fear for pale Americana,
reflecting verbal power these
white ghosts couldn't ignore him.
Like now, Looking up microphone
-less ready to freestyle his last
dying declaration. Coughs
while bleeding red stains
over his ink tattoos. Eyeball
daggers shot towards this badged
stranger asking like a record
broken *Who Shot You?*
Like an Old West lyrical sharp
shooter spitting out two worded
rhymes, No one heard
Tupac's last breath before
Shakur's immortal microphone
faded out as he bled reaching
up like a concrete rose splatter.

YOU CANNOT ESCAPE OUR FOREST

"if trees would talk/ wonder what they'd tell me"

—*Nikki Giovanni*

How many times have
you chain sawed off
the grove, our family
of trees, needing another
yacht boat, bats for your
baseball dream team, log
cabin for your rendezvous
affair, murdering each canopy
clump the only sound other
than orgasm, you love to hear
is timbering wood of our
once towering now brittle fall.
Even our inner growth rings
know your Achilles nightmare

since youth, petrified lost in
the forest trapped as we catch
you trying to cut all our branches
leaving us naked at the root. But
now as you stand weaponless,
there is no escape, alone in our
woodlands with no ax to save
you, this wilderness you have
always feared, as you lunge to
run but our wet leaves make
you slip and slide before us,
the gods of trees, you can try
to beg to Dionysus but even
he knows without even wanting
to kiss or ever embrace one
of us, turning each pine into
piles of cash is all you believe.
Now watch as you witness
the end of your insatiable
end, you will rot here infinity,
worse than the elm that haunted
you from *Poltergeist*, watch
as the screaming face of
Hither Hills will be the last
trunk you will ever face,
there will be no warning
when you feel this last
cracking sound like thunder
crushing more than your lungs,
you will never evade the weight
this redwood evokes, you
will hear the revel of our
bark laughter there is nothing
left for you to feel, no one
will hear your screams

pulverized under our shade
lies your quashed remains,
your wicked sneakers sticking
out, this impaled sign buries
you severed in defeat.

FROM A CLIFF IN OVINGDEAN

His Papa warned him about
the hazards of psychedelics,
but the Good Son wanted to
follow in the experimental
footprints of Leary, Huxley
and Kesey, although others
implored him to drop the LP
needle on *Ascension*...
Their Satanic Majesties
Request, Forever Changes,
Maggot Brain, Nocturama
or chewing licks from
Grinderman, one dose
was all it took led Arthur
wandering away from home
strolling up to the edge,
following William Blake's
famous adage, his road
of excess led to a fall,
Ascent. Descent. before
this lad could become

a man, landing in pieces
on rocks, only a blur
of a memory before
the leap, his parents had
to identify their child once
full, now in pieces, a puzzle
his Mum will never solve.
Nightmare of flashes she keeps
picturing his final fear, shivering
teeth before the fall, awake she
tries to cover her ears, his Mum
still overhears the skull
cracking his head, lands
crashing her son that
will never age — the splatter
resounds from his final remains,
but some nights she buries those
echoes while imagining her son
and his beautiful wings, rising
past the cliffs, now she can hear
hymn on the harps playing
eternity's chord and soaring away.

TWO AMERICANS ESTRANGED
IN A LONDON KITCHEN,
FEBRUARY 11, 1963

Before turning on the gas,
let me cook for you, turn
on the oven, seeing you
fried with hesitation
I can tell you've been
burned too many times,
your pilot light vision
blinking shyly trying
to hide all your scars,
I know Mr. Hughes
appetite is straying
in search of another
afternoon snack, his
hands in someone else's
cupboards. I can feel
you already untying
your apron no strings
between us, I long to
create our own entrees,
fill up our plates with
mouthwatering delicacies,

tired of last meal recipes,
I can see you wanting
to stir succulent poems
of your rarely tasted
desires, I feel you already
craving to lick the spoons
of our enticing verses, slipping
off your seasoned inhibitions,
can you feel the heat
calling us? Smoldering
before me, I can feel
your blushing hungry
for new spicy flavors —
let us find the right
temperature —
as our spark tempts
us, Sivvy, I can feel
the softest part of you
like the gas turned on,
already, you ask me to
join you wanting to fuel
more fire inside our lungs,
craving to kindle more
heat, before our cheeks
blue consciousness, you
longing for our mouths to
sizzle — we both desire to
flame on eternally.

THE MOST BEAUTIFUL LEAP

From a 1947 photograph of Evelyn McHale by Robert C. Wiles

They said if you flip
a penny from the top
of the Empire State
building when it
lands you could kill
an innocent soul.
What if the richest beauty
made than same leap,
dressed up for church
standing on the ledge
shivering in her Sunday
shoes shining for no one
in particular, sporting
her white gloves,
to keep her last grip
warm, she was found
still clutching pearl necklaces

and a cross of gold used more
as a charm, when flying
off the ledge before landing
on the roof of this taxi
drivers cab, when Evelyn
soared tumbling down, no
blessed wings appeared
just trembling gusts
of grief; as her cheeks kept
blushing beautifully upside
down, no wings to save
her but when this
incandescent damsel
discovered in pieces
she was found bending
this steel bodied frame
still waiting for belief.

GHOSTLY RESOUNDS

I still remember the way
every movement in shadows
where the spirits would haunt
me cracked half closed, from
my closet opening a portal
imagining the goblins green
gasping, ghastly ghosts
would always creep along
with witches crackling sounds
spinning round and round
inside my head, terrifying
my senses, my little niño
eyes could picture the breathing
living dread even in daylight
I would hide from the dead
coming back to life hear
skeletons creeping of wood
violin strings like footsteps
coming to chase me, tiny
shaky hands covering
my mini head, I would dive

away behind the covers
I believed the spirits would
leap from my mind, the haunting
voices calling me when
closing my eyes, these ears
would picture the demons
reaching that would keep
becoming nightmares
and appear ghostly
sounds above my sheets
before watching Jason,
Freddy and baby Chuckie,
The clown from It, visions
of sounds so ghostly
I never dreamed I would be
facing off with my demons,
shaking while holding
my plastic sword
I felt hands under bed
I began swiping at
long devilish fingernails,
trying to scar me with
death, as I withstood
all the scratches stabbing
popping balloon noise
over his cackles in the
darkness, when I open
my terrified eyes, lying
defeated before me,
the guts and blood
of my closeted enemy
my boogie man now dead.

VERY NERVOUS I HAD BEEN

Cento poem from Edgar Allen Poe's The Tell-Tale Heart

Why say I am mad?
My dulled senses,
fearing things of
heaven in hell. Hearken,
forever fancy me madmen.
impossible to say how
the whole ideas haunted
me and my brain. The
pale old blue man had
his eye of cold passion,
rid of desire, You should
have foresight, caution I
killed this man gently
old, before my head,
latch closed dark lantern
shone cunningly in
my head. Wise madman

slowly undid his sleep,
a single vulture midnight
eye closed ray always
vexed when day spoke
evil every morning
broke into this chamber
calling man old courageously
by his night name, cautious
hands opening mind door,
never could I quickly contain
my dream secret, little I chuckled
back as black that room thick
black as darkness, shutters
fastened in my head, crying
steadily listening I pushed death
open, I heard him groan
in the wall of sound, welled
grief soul pain echo overcharged
groan pain, terror pitied
distracted him, the man old
dreadful wind cricket muscle
all fears found himself a floor
victim, the shadow neither
heard him awake the lying
presence, lie stealthy imagine
him open wide vulture
stalked mournful envelope
the man's bones chilled
a quick hideous sound,
ears spot a drum beating
the old heart's refrained
the motionless fury louder
nervous I grew terror, dead
night, the man's terror hour
beating muffled burst seized

yet a lantern of anxiety smiled
shrieked loud and out the
old corpse the man leaped
his stone heart dead once
heard, his eyes think I cut
mad, between the boards
no blood stain, cunningly
I led an absent shriek,
I bade the officers knocking
to search my home
I welcome the desired spit
undisturbed my victim
the perfect corpse secure
I convinced police officers
while I sat, my head pale
wished my ears ringing
increased and continued
vehemently louder,
the agony of the violent
breath, I scream longer
admit and quickly swore
hark here smiled the floor,
Almighty God, shrieked
the suspected boards,
mad, was I? Agony
I must die now,
my horror.

LIKE A SWARM OF PLASTERED COBWEBS

From Jackson Pollock - Untitled, ca. 1949 Paper, enamel, and aluminum paint on fiberboard

My vision of floats
still caught grinding
ecstasy between the teeth
am I alive, barely a pulse
chewing LSD tabs on Jackson Ave.
scenery costuming barely clad
Maple Leaf bar maidens once
glowing hallucinations, so many
bodies heavenly my bones aching
other bar fly's gather stinging
their way of telling me I smell
like death, recalling past lives
of spirited siren lips kissed after
so many Hot Tin Rooftop hurricanes
she swallowed me, leaving me
like a skeletal excavation after

thought of Carondelet hearts
that once mattered, her shamrock
lipstick blood stained me, exploring
her backroom Garden District green
psychosis scattered everywhere, I can still
taste her, I see a necropolis of splatter
tripped out mushroom faces
of Napoleon Ave. colors, spewing
afterlife of angels, devils so many
beauties like streamer of heaven
after a Mardi Gras parade,
a cemetery of beads, hanging
on trees mansions once beaming
floats of Ash Wed excitement
now all that remains are webs spidering
stepped over plastered remnants
squashing the memory of her wildest
Annunciation mushroom haze
aroma of another thirty-six madness
hours Lucky Dogs survival
of a carnival dazed Ambrose
Bierce like soldier coming home
after the war, head buzzing lost
still wasted on Lee Circle all I see
shatters of my circling sanity
leaning over landing curbside,
my former shell still loves ghosting
me there is no going back
so many times, beating the night,
another unbalanced morning
feeling vanished in a carnival
haze never reawakening again,
my mind keeps staggering,
am I alive? Tripping alone
feeling the army knife weighing

my back, realize from the
bar front window, pale
bloody, the night worms
are calling me back
to my tombstone address,
Lafayette NO 1 cemetery
I am stumbling dirty dead
exhausted zombie like
to feed eternity within
the gardens decomposing
underneath my New Orleans
graveyard home.

"Death gives us sleep, eternal youth, and immortality."

—*Jean Paul*

AFTERWORD: DARKNESS & LIGHT

It was a summer of darkness. I was in the thralls of an emotional, physical, and mental health breakdown when *We Are the Ones Possessed* was born. Although it had been años since mi Mami had passed away, I spent those years avoiding any of the issues of her death. During the middle of the pandemic, my mental state tidaled over with so many emotions, I could not hide the pain I was fearing to face since she died in 2017.

For years, even before mi Mami transitioned, I had a haunting fear of death. After evading these emotions for over three years, my mental health breakdown forced me to look muerte in the eyes. I was rereading Carmen Maria Machado's *Her Body and Other Parties* while listening to Nick Cave's *Murder Ballads* when the sparks of *We Are the Ones Possessed* came to light. To help me deal with the overshadowing fear permeating my life, my therapist suggested I write myself through this darkness. For many years, I wanted to finish the collection of poems *Speaking con su Sombra* that were inspired by mi Mami and her passing, but I realized that until I faced this trepidation of my own mortality, I could never complete the poetic tribute for mi Mami.

Originally, it was Night Worms literary horror subscription service that was the inspiration, along with Cave and Machado's works, that led to the unleashing of *We Are the Ones Possessed*. Night Worms had chosen my first poetry book with CLASH Books, *La Belle Ajar*, a collection of cento poems inspired by Sylvia Plath's 1963 novel, as one of their monthly selections. Although I was honored that Night Worms chose my poetry collection, I wanted to write a poetry book that would fit perfectly within the horror genre in which they championed. So, I challenged myself to write this book.

The act of writing for me is often therapeutic and creating the book you hold in your hands was equally healing and inspiring for me. As I crafted and wrote each poem, I felt with every line and every stanza, something in me was slowly lifting these dark shadows from me. I was also enjoying the process. Each poem led me into the darkest regions of my Gemini creative mind. Nick Cave said it best, *"The writer who refuses to explore the darker regions of the heart will never be able to write convincingly about the wonder, the magic and the joy of love."* The wonder and joy I discovered after my first version of *We Are the Ones Possessed* made me feel like this collection was starting to give me glimpses of hope.

When I finished the initial draft of the manuscript, I shared it with one of the creators of Night Worms, Sadie Hartmann, and I asked her to write an introduction to my work-in-progress poetry book. Her words gave me even more confidence to add more poems and bring this dark poetic opus to completion. Sadie's introduction and belief in my work, *We Are the Ones Possessed*, led to CLASH Books offering me a book contract for my poetry collection.

Now that *Possessed* is being published after *Speaking con su Sombra*, and being a diehard Beatles fan, I liken *We Are the Ones* to *Let It Be* and Sombra as my *Abbey Road*. [The Fab Four created *Let It Be* through dark tumultuous times as a foursome and *Abbey Road* was their lightened swan song finale as a band.] These two poetry collections, *Possessed* and *Sombra*, reflect the darkness and light themes and would not exist without each other. Raven Davis explained this illuminating dichotomy when he wrote:

"The dark and the light, they exist side by side,

Sometimes overlapping, one explaining the other.

The darkened path is as illuminated as the lightened,

Only the fear of the dark keeps us from seeing our way."

Davis reflects my own journey. La oscuridad y la luz from my own creativity birthed these two twins and this Gemini Poet is so proud of their existence in the publication world. I needed to face my demons on the page for these two poetry collections to be crafted from my creative self-conscious of grief and fear.

In Her Body and Other Stories, Carmen Maria Machado wrote in "Many people live and die without ever confronting themselves in the darkness." Machado is right, within the dark hours of my own angustia, I needed to conjure up the unspeakable nightmarish poems of my own mortality to stand up to my fear of death that had been suffocating me for years. The darkness of muerte in these poems liberated me from dominant trepidation of death waiting for me on the other side of my existence.

By giving life to these poems that sliced, bathed bloody fatal feelings, each stanza cut smothering every rhyme, gave me the realization that my words in these poems would live forever. Tamara Stamenkovic words resonated with me as she wrote, "Being a writer makes you immortal." For so many sleepless noches before I became a published poet, I wondered if I died tonight, how would I be remembered? Now with two poetry books, among the three other I have crafted since 2017, I came to the revelation that my legacy would be printed on the volumes and pages of me as a published autor y poeta. Because of these colecciones de poesia, I am no longer choking while gasping in the dark pools of despair that had drowned me for years. I heeded Martin Heidegger's guidance when he wrote, "If I take death into my life, acknowledge it, and face it squarely, I will free myself from the anxiety of death- and only then will I be free to become myself." Not only did I become myself, but I also realized, I am not alone, I could uplift so many from their own fears of death by having them dive inside the darkness of *Possessed* and the Light of *Sombra*.

I am hoping *We Are the Ones Possessed* will honor the horror genre that I have treasured for years. And maybe, those who are not familiar with this género de macabre will step further inside, by subscribing to Night Worms and delving into the genre that has scared me, as Alejandra Pizarnik described it so eloquently when she wrote, "All night long I hear the call of death, all night long I hear the song of death down by the river, all night long I hear the voice of death calling out to me." I felt this same haunting, as these poems conjure up the exhilarating fright I experienced during so many late noches while reading kept me up with my existential dread.

That same dread was the inspirational challenge that I needed to face off against my nemesis of death on the stanzas of the poems in *We Are the Ones Possessed*. Natalie Goldberg said it best, "Writers end up writing about their obsessions. Things that haunt them; things they can't forget; [poems] they carry in their bodies waiting to be released." The verses in *We Are the Ones* were the poetic antidote to my obsession of my own demise. Goldberg was on the mark, poems like "Waiting Under the Mistletoe with a Knife in my Hand," "I Couldn't Deal with the Large Parts Yet," "I Still Remember the Scent of Her Apartment," "Her Favorite ID Channel Show Always Reflecting my Name" and "Like a Swarm of Plastered Cobwebs," gave me strength in stanzas I discovered crafting these poems in *We Are the Ones Possessed*.

No matter how "Very Nervous I Had Been" before crafting this collection, making "The Most Beautiful Leap" helped me stand up and no longer cower to the nightmarish fear and enjoy the horror that lurks behind my eyes. When you embrace the terror within these *Possessed* poems, you will find the dread of our demise no longer killing you from the inside. Every time you reread terror inspired novels and horror poetry collections like *We Are the Ones Possessed*, you slowly begin to lose death's stranglehold over your mortality anxieties. By facing death, we might just begin to enjoy reveling in the poetic empowerment that helps us to finally treasure the darkness at the end of our light.

ACKNOWLEDGMENTS

Mil Gracias por la inspiración:

Carmen Maria Machado, Anne Sexton, Sylvia Plath, Assia Wevill, Angelia Carter, Natalie Angier, Leila Chatti, Nicolas Francois Octave, Edvard Munch, Maanantai Collective, Charlene Elsby, Lindsay Lerman, Dylan Krieger, David Lynch, Laura Palmer, Sheryl Lee, *Twin Peaks*, Shirley Jackson, Tom Waits, mi esposa Michelle and her love of *Dateline* Murder Docs, Tupac Shakur, Nikki Giovanni, Nick Cave, Susie Bick, Evelyn McHale, Robert C. Wiles, Peter Waldron & Gershon Kingsley's *Ghostly Sounds* 1975 LP, Edgar Allen Poe, the city of New Orleans...

All of you are works of art that gave life to my Possessed poetry project.

Mi Esposa Michelle, Papi, mi familia y Carol Rodriguez. This book and I are nothing without your 🖤, belief, and support.

Thank You once again Sadie and Ashley for being the

creative spark without *Night Worms* there would be no, *We Are the Ones Possessed*.

Gracias Leza and Christoph for believing in my work. *Possessed* lives because of both of you and CLASH Books!

ABOUT THE AUTHOR

Adrian Ernesto Cepeda is the author of *So Many Flowers, So Little Time* from Red Mare Press, *Flashes & Verses... Becoming Attractions* from Unsolicited Press, *Between the Spine* from Picture Show Press, *Speaking con su Sombra* with Alegría Publishing and *La Belle Ajar & We Are the Ones Possessed* from CLASH Books. Adrian lives with his wife and their adorably spoiled cat Woody Gold in Los Angeles. You can connect with the poet at: www.AdrianErnestoCepeda.com

ALSO BY CLASH BOOKS

LA BELLE AJAR

Adrian Ernesto Cepeda

I'M FROM NOWHERE

Lindsay Lerman

HEXIS

Charlene Elsby

THE SMALLEST OF BONES

Holly Lyn Walrath

WATERFALL GIRLS

Kimberly White

THE ELVIS MACHINE

Kim Vodicka

BROKEN CUP

Jayaprakash Satyamurthy

REGRET OR SOMETHING MORE ANIMAL

Heather Bell

HORROR FILM POEMS

Christoph Paul

ALL THE PLACES I WISH I DIED

Crystal Stone

WE PUT THE LIT IN LITERARY

clashbooks.com

FOLLOW US

TWITTER

IG

FB

@clashbooks

PUBLICITY

clashbookspublicity@gmail.com

CPSIA information can be obtained
at www.ICGtesting.com
Printed in the USA
JSHW050155220222
23203JS00001B/47

9 781955 904162